Bugs, Bugs, Bugs

Richard Tan

Rosen REAL READERS

Rosen Classroom™
New York

A dragonfly flies.

An ant has six legs.

This butterfly is black and blue.

A ladybug has spots.

A snail lives in a shell.

A bee has stripes.

Words To Know

ant

bee

butterfly

dragonfly

ladybug

snail